World of Reptiles

Pythons

by Matt Doeden

Consultant:
The Staff of Reptile Gardens
Rapid City, South Dakota

Mankato, Minnesota

Bridgestone Books are published by Capstone Press,
151 Good Counsel Drive, P.O. Box 669, Mankato, Minnesota 56002.
www.capstonepress.com

Library of Congress Cataloging-in-Publication Data
Doeden, Matt.
  Pythons / by Matt Doeden.
    p. cm.—(Bridgestone books. World of reptiles)
  Includes bibliographical references and index.
  ISBN 0-7368-3733-7 (hardcover)
  1. Pythons—Juvenile literature. I. Title. II. Series: World of reptiles.
QL666.O67D63 2005
597.96'78—dc22   2004014481

Editorial Credits

Heather Adamson, editor; Enoch Peterson, designer; Ted Williams, cover designer; Erin Scott,
    illustrator; Jo Miller, photo researcher; Scott Thoms, photo editor

Photo Credits

Allen Blake Sheldon, cover
Brand X Pictures, 1
Bruce Coleman Inc./Joe McDonald, 4, 20; Michael Fogden, 6; John Giustina, 18
James E. Gerholdt, 10
McDonald Wildlife Photography/Joe McDonald, 16
Photo Researchers, Inc./Science Photo Library/Peter Chadwick, 12

1 2 3 4 5 6 10 09 08 07 06 05

Table of Contents

Pythons

What animal hangs from trees, swims in water, and hides in grass? What's the longest snake ever measured? It's the python.

Pythons are reptiles. Like most reptiles, they have scales and hatch from eggs. Reptiles are also **cold-blooded**. They depend on their surroundings for their body heat.

Pythons are **constricting** snakes. They do not have fangs. They squeeze their **prey** to death. Anacondas and boa constrictors also kill prey by squeezing.

◄ Shiny scales cover the body of this reticulated python.

What Pythons Look Like

Some pythons are among the longest snakes in the world. Reticulated pythons grow to 20 feet (6 meters) long. Other pythons are much smaller. Pygmy pythons rarely grow longer than 2 feet (60 centimeters).

Smooth, shiny scales cover a python's body. The scales can be many different colors. A python's color depends on where it lives. Pythons that live in trees are the color of green vines. Pythons that live on the ground are colored like fallen leaves.

◄ Pythons have colors that blend with their surroundings. This scrub python hides on fallen leaves.

Pythons Range Map

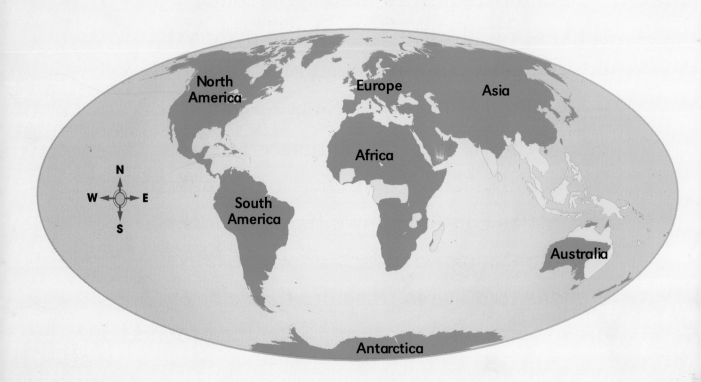

☐ Where Pythons Live

Pythons in the World

Pythons live in warm areas. Some live in tropical rain forests. Others live in deserts or grasslands.

Pythons live in many different places around the world. Many pythons live in India and other parts of Asia. Some pythons, such as rock pythons, live in Africa. Carpet pythons and other pythons live in Australia.

◄ About 20 types of pythons live throughout the world.

Python Habitats

Most pythons live on the ground. They usually stay near plants in their warm habitats. They rest in the shade. They hide as they wait for prey.

Some pythons live in trees. They wrap their tails around branches and watch for prey. Other pythons, such as black-headed pythons, live in underground holes.

◀ This ball python lives on the ground and watches for prey.

What Pythons Eat

Pythons eat many kinds of prey. Small pythons eat fish, lizards, frogs, and rats. Large pythons hunt wild pigs, deer, sheep, and goats. A few pythons have even eaten people.

Pythons do not usually chase prey. Instead, they pick a hiding spot and wait for prey to come near.

Pythons are constrictors. When pythons catch an animal, they wrap their bodies around the prey. They squeeze until the prey cannot breathe and **suffocates**.

◄ Large pythons like this African rock python, swallow deer and other large prey headfirst.

Life Cycle of a Python

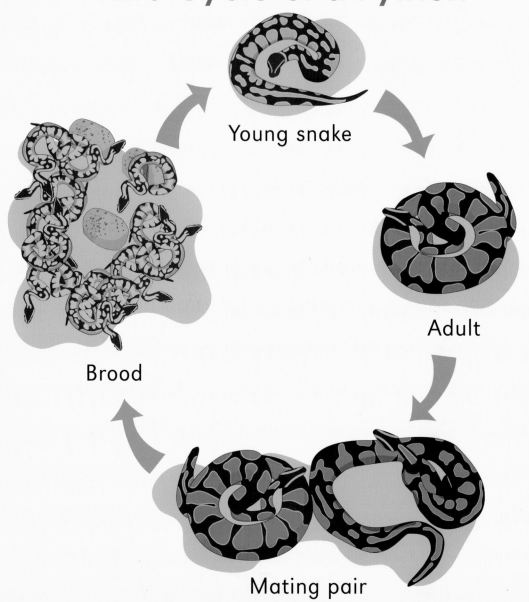

Young snake

Adult

Mating pair

Brood

Producing Young

Pythons live and hunt alone. They gather only to **mate**. After mating, most pythons do not stay together.

The female python guards the eggs. She wraps her body around the eggs to keep them warm. The female may stay with the eggs for three months or more. Once the snakes hatch, the female leaves.

A python nest may have from five to more than 100 eggs. A group of young pythons is called a brood.

Growing Up

Young pythons are about 18 to 24 inches (46 to 61 centimeters) long when they hatch. Young pythons must survive on their own after they hatch. They do not stay in the nest. They hunt and take care of themselves.

Young pythons grow fast. They shed their skin, or **molt**, as they get longer. Pythons molt several times each year. Young pythons molt more often than adults.

◀ As soon as pythons break free from their soft egg shells, they are ready to live on their own.

Dangers to Pythons

Adult pythons have few natural **predators**. Crocodiles and eagles may eat young pythons. Most animals do not attack giant snakes.

People are the biggest danger to pythons. Pythons move slowly, so they are easy to kill. People hunt pythons for their meat and their skins. People catch them to sell as pets.

People also harm python habitats. As forests are cut down, pythons have less room to live and hunt. Some kinds of pythons are in danger of dying out.

◄ Crocodiles are one of the few animals that may make meals of pythons.

Amazing Facts about Pythons

- Some people keep pythons as pets. The ball python is a popular pet snake because it grows only to about 5 feet (1.5 meters) long.

- Pythons are good swimmers. They can even swim in the ocean.

- Female pythons sometimes shiver as they sit on their eggs. Shivering raises their body temperature and warms the eggs.

- Green tree pythons are bright red or yellow when they first hatch. The colors match the flowers in the trees where pythons rest.

◄ Young green tree pythons are not green. They start out red or yellow and change to green as they get older.

Glossary

cold-blooded (KOHLD-BLUHD-id)—having a body temperature that is the same as the surroundings; all reptiles are cold-blooded.

constrict (kuhn-STRIKT)—to squeeze; a python constricts its body to suffocate prey.

mate (MATE)—to join together to produce young

molt (MOHLT)—to shed an outer layer of skin

predator (PRED-uh-tur)—an animal that hunts other animals for food

prey (PRAY)—an animal hunted for food

suffocate (SUHF-uh-kate)—to die from having no air; a python's prey suffocates from being squeezed so tight that it cannot breathe.

Read More

Murray, Julie. *Pythons.* A Buddy Book. Edina, Minn.: Abdo, 2003.

Weber, Valerie J. *Reticulated Pythons.* World's Largest Snakes. Milwaukee: Gareth Stevens, 2003.

Internet Sites

FactHound offers a safe, fun way to find Internet sites related to this book. All of the sites on FactHound have been researched by our staff.

Here's how:
1. Visit *www.facthound.com*
2. Type in this special code **0736837337** for age-appropriate sites. Or enter a search word related to this book for a more general search.
3. Click on the **Fetch It** button.

FactHound will fetch the best sites for you!

Index